A Note to Parents and Teachers

DK READERS is a compelling reading programme for children, designed in conjunction with leading literacy experts, including Cliff Moon M.Ed., Honorary Fellow of the University of Reading. Cliff Moon has spent many years as a teacher and teacher educator specializing in reading and has written more than 160 books for children and teachers. He is series editor to Collins Big Cat.

Beautiful illustrations and superb full-colour photographs combine with engaging, easy-to-read stories to offer a fresh approach to each subject in the series. Each DK READER is guaranteed to capture a child's interest while developing his or her reading skills, general knowledge, and love of reading.

The five levels of DK READERS are aimed at different reading abilities, enabling you to choose the books that are exactly right for your child:

Pre-level 1: Learning to read
Level 1: Beginning to read
Level 2: Beginning to read alone
Level 3: Reading alone
Level 4 Proficient readers

The "normal" age at which a child begins to read can be anywhere from three to eight years old. Adult participation through the lower levels is very helpful for providing encouragement, discussing storylines and sounding out unfamiliar words.

No matter which level you select, you can be sure that you are helping your child learn to read, then read to learn!

Illustrator Peter Dennis
Jacket Designer Mary Sandberg

Subject Consultant Louis Carlat
Thomas A. Edison Papers

Reading Consultant
Cliff Moon, M.Ed.

Published in Great Britain by
Dorling Kindersley Limited,
80 Strand, London WC2R 0RL

A CIP record for this book is available
from the British Library

ISBN: 978-1-4053-2145-7

Colour reproduction by Colourscan, Singapore
Printed and bound in China by L Rex Printing Co., Ltd.

The publisher would like to thank the following for their kind permission
to reproduce their photographs:
(Key: a-above; b-below/bottom; c-centre; l-left; r-right; t-top)

Alamy Images: Eye Candy Images 39crb; **Corbis:** 12b, 22cl, 23br, 40cl; Bettmann 3, 4cla,
10clb, 15t, 20-21b, 24br, 28bl, 34clb, 34tl, 37b, 40tl, 43b; W. Dickson 10tl; Historical
Picture Archive 7cr; Hulton-Deutsch Collection 26tl; John Springer Collection 41tr;
Michael Keller 4-5b; Patrice Latron 46bl; Schenectady Museum, Hall of Electrical History
Foundation 5tr, 23tr, 25t, 30b, 33tr; Joseph Sohm / Visions of America 36bl; Underwood &
Underwood 44bl; **DK Images:** Science Museum, London 6bl, 7tr, 12tl, 24cr (light bulbs),
27tr, 31tr, 39tr, 49b; **The Edison Papers / Rutgers, The State University of New Jersey:**
4bl, 15br, 17ca, 17tr, 23tl, 32b; **U.S. Department of the Interior, National Park Service,
Edison National Historic Site:** 6tl, 8tl, 9cra, 14bl, 16b, 16tl, 18clb, 20clb, 20tl, 21tr, 29t,
41bl, 41cr, 42cla, 45br; **Getty Images:** Max Dannenbaum / The Image Bank 47t; **Mary
Evans Picture Library:** 33crb; **Science & Society Picture Library:** NMPFT 38tl, 38-39b;
Science Museum 19tr; **Science Photo Library:** Alex Bartel 25cr; Humanities & Social
Sciences Library / New York Public Library 36tl; Library Of Congress 37cr; Jerry Schad 24tl

Jacket images: Front: **Alamy Images:** Jeff Greenberg (b/g); **SuperStock:** b. Back: **Alamy
Images:** Visual Arts Library (London) tr; **Corbis:** Michael Freeman tl

All other images © Dorling Kindersley
For more information see: www.dkimages.com

Discover more at
www.dk.com

Contents

READERS

PROFICIENT **4** READERS

Thomas Edison
The Great Inventor

Written by Caryn Jenner

A Dorling Kindersley Book

This poster shows Thomas Edison with many of his most celebrated inventions.

Legal patent
A patent gives legal ownership of an invention. No one can use the idea without permission from the inventor.

The genius of Edison

Look around. Do you see electric lights or appliances plugged into electric sockets? Have you listened to music or seen a film lately?

Many of the things we now take for granted are thanks to the inventions of Thomas Alva Edison. Edison had patents on 1,093 inventions, including the phonograph, the incandescent light bulb, the film camera and an entire system of bringing electricity into our homes. This book describes a few of his most important inventions.

Edison aimed to invent things that people would use.

Edison's patent for autographic printing, dated 8 August, 1876

4

He researched his ideas and experimented – usually for many years – until his inventions were ready to manufacture and sell. Often, he and other inventors improved on each other's work. Edison considered himself an inventor and a businessman.

Edison was full of ideas, but he was also a hard worker. He said, "Genius is one percent inspiration and 99 percent perspiration."

Edison at work
Edison had the determination and persistence to turn his ideas into working inventions. "I make trial after trial until it comes," he said.

Thomas Alva Edison was born in 1847 in the small town of Milan, Ohio. When he was growing up, steam power was thought to be modern technology. Electricity was a mystery and the practical uses for it were just starting to be explored.

Birthplace
Edison's childhood home in Milan, Ohio, is now a museum. The family moved to Port Huron, Michigan, in 1854, when Edison was seven years old.

Steam power
The force of expanding and contracting steam can be used to power machines like this steam locomotive.

Since ancient times, people had been aware of the existence of electricity. However, it was not until 1820 that Danish scientist Hans Christian Oersted discovered that an electric current could make a magnetized needle move.

Now scientists realised that electricity could be used to power machines. British scientist Michael Faraday researched this and his work would later influence a young Thomas Edison.

To Edison, electricity was a practical, efficient source of power for many of his inventions. He imagined that his inventions would change the world and he worked to make his vision a reality.

Electro-magnetism
Oersted used this apparatus to show the magnetic effects of an electric current flowing in a wire. His discovery is the basis for today's electric machines.

Faraday
In 1831, Faraday discovered how to turn an electric current on and off by manipulating a magnetic field.

Trains and telegraphs

Young Edison
Edison was the youngest of seven children, but three of them died in childhood. His surviving brother and two sisters were much older than him.

1855 Eight-year-old Thomas Alva Edison raised his hand.

"Sir, may I ask a question?"

"You ask too many questions, Edison," bellowed the teacher.

"But, sir . . ."

"Quiet, Al. You'll get into trouble," whispered the boy next to him.

It was too late.

"What an addled boy you are, Edison!" shouted the teacher.

Edison knew that addled meant confused and stupid, and he was neither. He burst into tears and ran out of the schoolroom and all the way home to tell his mother.

As a young child, Edison had been ill with scarlet fever, so he had only recently started school. But he kept fidgeting and asking questions, which made the teacher angry.

When he told his mother, she insisted on seeing the teacher.

"Mrs. Edison," the teacher sighed, "your son is a difficult boy."

"Sir, Al has a very curious mind, but it is clear that he is not learning a great deal from you," she declared. "I was once a schoolteacher myself, and I shall now take over my son's education. Good day, sir."

Edison's father
Samuel Ogden Edison Jr. was a small businessman whose business ventures sometimes failed, causing financial difficulties.

Edison's mother
Edison said of his mother, Nancy Elliot Edison, "My mother was the making of me. She was so true, so sure of me, and I felt I had someone to live for, someone I must not disappoint."

Child labour
Like many children of the time, Edison worked. Children often had jobs on farms or in factories.

In the news
Edison's newspapers were full of news about the American Civil War (1861-1865) that divided the country between North and South.

Edison's mother encouraged him to explore and learn on his own. He studied history, ancient myths and the plays of Shakespeare.

He didn't like maths but was fascinated by science and he experimented in a small laboratory at home.

Edison was partially deaf, possibly due to the scarlet fever he had as a child. In later years, he said that being hard of hearing helped him concentrate because he wasn't distracted by the noises around him.

At age 12, Edison sold newspapers and snacks on the steam trains between Port Huron, Michigan, and the city of Detroit. News reports from other states were sent via telegraph wires to offices at the main railway stations. Eventually, Edison published his own newspapers using these reports and sold them on the train.

In his spare time on the train, he read scientific books and did experiments in a small laboratory that he set up in the baggage car. One day, Edison accidentally started a fire in the car. No one was hurt, but the angry conductor threw him off the train.

Steam train
When the first steam railway in the United States of America opened in 1831, travel around the vast country became quicker and easier.

Telegraph
The electric telegraph began to be used in 1837, greatly improving communication across long distances. Like railway tracks, telegraph wires soon criss-crossed the country.

11

Telegrapher
A telegrapher used Morse code to tap out a message, sending electrical signals along the wires. A telegrapher at the receiving end then decoded the message.

Morse code
In Morse code, each letter of the alphabet is represented by dots and dashes. These are transmitted as short and long signals, and can be heard as clicks on the telegraph receiver.

1862 One day, Edison saw a small boy playing on the train track, right in the path of an approaching freight car!

"Look out!" Edison shouted. He dashed across the track, scooped the boy up, and quickly carried him to safety.

This engraving from 1879 shows Edison carrying the stationmaster's son to safety.

The boy was the son of the stationmaster. As a reward for saving his son's life, the stationmaster taught Edison to send and receive telegraph messages in Morse code – the system of dots and dashes used in telegraphy. Soon, Edison became an expert telegrapher.

At age 16, he began travelling around Canada and the United States, working as a telegrapher in different cities. Edison also invented ways to improve the telegraph. The Morse "repeater", for example, recorded the dots and dashes so they could be repeated later at a slower speed. This helped telegraphers decode long messages more accurately. However, his employer, Western Union, thought decoding messages with the Morse repeater was too slow.

Changing nation
Edison travelled at a time of great change in America. The Civil War ended in 1865 and the nation was rebuilding. Meanwhile, settlers continued to move westwards and form new states.

■ Union states
□ Territories
■ Confederate states

Western Union
Established in 1856, Western Union was the largest telegraph company in the United States.

Edison the inventor

Electric vote recorder
Edison invented the electric vote recorder specifically for use by lawmakers. When voting for or against a proposal, they flipped a switch on the recorder to indicate "yes" or "no" and the votes were counted automatically.

1868 Edison moved between cities and jobs. He was sacked several times because the telegraph companies wanted "operators, not experimenters". At age 21, he became a full-time inventor.

He received his first patent in 1869 for the electric vote recorder. A friend tried to sell it to the United States Congress in Washington, D.C., but they said, "If there is any invention on earth that we don't need, this is it." They liked voting slowly in case they wanted to change their minds.

Disappointed, Edison decided that he would only invent "what the public wants". He thought it was pointless inventing something that didn't sell.

Edison decided to move to New York City. He became interested in the New York Stock Exchange, where investors bought and sold company shares. Edison used telegraph technology to improve the stock ticker – a machine that transmitted the constantly changing share prices. Edison sold the patent for his improved stock ticker and some related inventions to Western Union for $40,000 (£7,100).

Mary Stilwell
At age 16, Mary Stilwell worked at Edison's new telegraph factory. After a brief courtship, the 24-year-old Edison married her.

First factory
Edison set up his factory and laboratory in Newark, New Jersey, close to New York City. Over the next few years, his staff grew to more than 250 people.

1871 With the money, Edison set up his own factory to make stock printers, and a laboratory where he continued work on the telegraph.

On Christmas Day, he married Mary Stilwell, one of his employees. They had three children, Marion, Thomas Jr. and William. Although he nicknamed Marion and Thomas Jr. "Dot" and "Dash" after the Morse code signals, Edison didn't spend much time with his family. He was usually in his laboratory, and often even fell asleep there.

Edison invented the quadruplex telegraph in 1874. It could send and receive four messages at the same time – twice as many as previous machines.

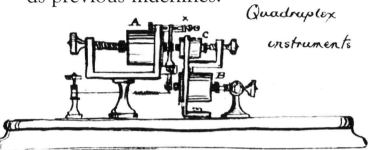

Quadruplex instruments

Electric pen
Edison invented the electric pen after recognising that businesses needed to copy documents. It was the forerunner of the photocopier.

In 1875, he invented the electric pen. It had a small, motorised needle attached to make a stencil of the document being written. The document could then be copied using an ink press.

During some experiments, Edison noticed mysterious sparks, which suggested that electricity could travel without wires. He called this "etheric force". Other scientists later used his observation as a basis for the investigation of radio waves.

Wireless
In the 1890s, Gugliemo Marconi used Edison's "etheric force" to send telegraph messages without wires. This was the beginning of long-distance radio communication.

The invention factory

1876 Profits from the factory paid for Edison's experiments, but running it distracted him from inventing.

He wrote, "I have innumerable machines in my mind now which I shall continue to illustrate and describe . . ." Throughout his life, he kept careful notes and drawings of his ideas.

Edison built a bigger laboratory in the New Jersey countryside at Menlo Park. He hired staff to manage his factory and accountants to manage the money, leaving him free to invent.

Edison boasted that he and his highly skilled engineering team at Menlo Park would have "a minor invention every ten days and a big thing every six months or so." In the first two years, they received 32 patents for their inventions.

Taking notes
During his lifetime, Edison filled more than 3,500 notebooks. He made sketches and notes for his inventions, and often even recorded the weather and what he ate.

Menlo Park
Inside the main laboratory at Menlo Park, Edison's staff were expected to work hard. However, Edison always worked harder but he also had a sense of fun.

Edison's first task was to improve the telephone that Alexander Graham Bell had invented earlier that year. Bell's telephone sent people's voices down the wires, but it only worked across short distances. Edison used carbon particles – very finely powdered black soot – in the transmitter to make the electrical current stronger. Voices now came through the wires loud and clear, even across long distances.

Bell's telephone Sound waves from voices cause vibrations that generate varying electric signals in the telephone transmitter. Vibrations in the receiver change the signals back to voice sounds.

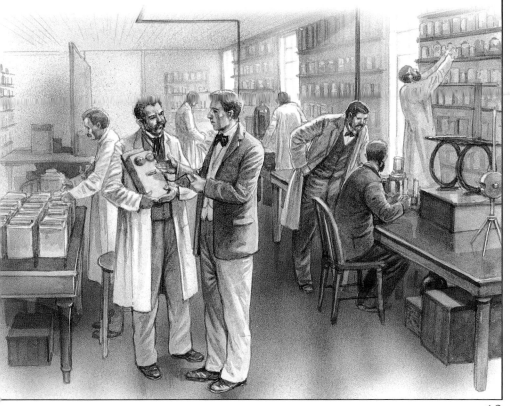

Two of Edison's staff

Kruesi
Edison gave sketches of his inventions to John Kruesi, who then built the devices. The phonograph was one of many inventions made by Kruesi.

Batchelor
Charles Batchelor spent long hours in the laboratory experimenting alongside Edison.

1877 Whilst experimenting with a new machine to record telegraph signals, Edison heard an unexpected sound as he pulled strips of paper rapidly under a needle. Based on this, he began to imagine a machine that could record voices. He set about designing a new device that would be able "to store up and reproduce automatically, at any future time, the human voice perfectly."

One December evening, Edison's staff gathered to watch a test. His new phonograph recorded onto a metal cylinder wrapped in tinfoil.

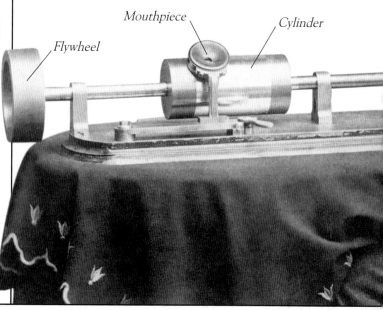

Mouthpiece
Cylinder
Flywheel

His staff doubted that a machine could record the human voice. Even Edison himself was secretly unsure.

He sang the nursery rhyme "Mary Had a Little Lamb" into the machine. Everyone was quiet as he turned the crank to play it back.

Suddenly, they heard, "Mary had a . . ."

It was Edison's voice, coming from the phonograph!

Crank

Phonograph
The word *phonograph* is taken from Greek words meaning "sound-writer". Edison later said that when he heard his voice on the phonograph, "I never was so taken aback in my life. Everybody was astonished. I was always afraid of things that worked the first time."

Favourite invention
In later life, Edison said the phonograph was his favourite invention. It was one of the few inventions that was entirely his own idea and not an improvement on someone else's.

Business tool
Edison thought that businesses could use his phonograph to record letters and telephone messages. He saw it as an early form of dictaphone and telephone answering machine.

The day after the successful demonstration at the lab, Edison recorded a message on the phonograph. He then took it to the offices of *Scientific American* – an important magazine for scientists.

Edison set up the phonograph on the editor's desk as curious employees gathered around. When he turned the crank, the phonograph spoke. It asked the astonished magazine editors if they were all impressed by Edison's new invention. They were!

In January 1878, Edison demonstrated an improved version of the phonograph in New York City. The public was amazed. More demonstrations took place all over America and Great Britain during the following months. Some people even fainted on hearing Edison's speaking phonograph.

At the age of 31, Edison became known as "The Wizard of Menlo Park".

Edison originally intended the phonograph to be used in businesses – to dictate letters, or as an early telephone answering machine. But he discovered that the success of the phonograph came largely from its use in travelling shows, which were a popular form of entertainment.

In April 1878, President Rutherford B. Hayes invited Edison to demonstrate the phonograph at the White House. Hayes was so delighted when he heard his own voice played back that he woke his sleeping wife so she could have a turn, too!

Travelling shows
Travelling circuses and shows exhibited the phonograph as a high-tech curiosity. These popular shows provided entertainment for people across America.

Switching on the light

1878 During a trip to see the eclipse of the sun, Edison and a friend discussed using electric current to make artificial light. Edison was so inspired, he later said, "This electric light idea took possession of me."

Two main types of artificial light were already in use. Gas lamps were often unreliable and dangerous. Arc lights, lit by an electric spark, were suitable for street lamps but far too bright for use in the home. Edison's alternative was an incandescent (glowing) light bulb that glowed from the heat of an electric current. He was confident that he could succeed where others had failed.

Solar eclipse
A solar eclipse occurs when the moon comes between Earth and the sun, blocking the sun.

Arc lighting
An electric arc light used two conductors to create an electric spark in the air that was dazzingly bright.

Edison announced to the press that he would invent not only a practical, long-lasting incandescent light bulb, but also a complete system of electric lighting for everyday use, with a supply network to bring electricity from the generator into people's homes. He would also have to design equipment, such as wires, circuits, switches and sockets.

Undaunted by the work ahead, Edison dreamt of a world lit up by electricity.

Gas lamps
By the 1870s, gas was piped along streets and into homes as fuel for lights. However, gas was expensive and there was a risk of gas explosions.

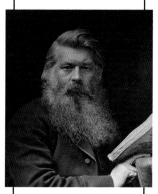

Joseph Swan
In England, Joseph Swan was already experimenting with incandescent light bulbs, but they didn't burn long enough and used too much current to be practical.

Lampblack
Edison had previously used lampblack as the source for the tiny carbon particles used in his telephone transmitter.

Edison's first challenge was to find the right material for the filament – the part inside the light bulb that would glow. Different materials burned at different rates, and in experiment after experiment they either burned out, melted or didn't glow at all.

"They're not failures," Edison said of his experiments. "They taught me something that I didn't know. They taught me what direction to move in."

In October 1879, Edison hit upon the idea of trying lampblack – the carbon, or black soot, found on the inside of lanterns. He and his team tried making small coils of carbon, but it didn't hold together. Then Edison burned pieces of cotton thread into carbon in a hot oven.

Edison inserted the carbonised thread into the glass bulb and switched on the electric current.

The light bulb shone for longer than Edison expected. To his delight, it was also only using a small amount of electric current.

"The longer it burned, the more fascinated we were," said Edison. "None of us could go to bed."

Filament

Glass bulb

How a light bulb works
When an electric current flows through the filament inside a light bulb, the filament becomes so hot that it glows.

The bulb must be vacuum-sealed, so that it contains no air. Otherwise, any air in the bulb would cause the filament to burn out.

Direct current (DC) generator
A DC generator, or dynamo, makes an electric current that flows in one direction only.

Nikola Tesla
In the late 1880s, a former employee of Edison's, Nikola Tesla, invented a motor that used alternating current (AC), which could be distributed more cheaply over longer distances than direct current.

Edison and his team made a small version of his electric light system at Menlo Park. It was powered by Edison's specially designed direct current (DC) generator. Incandescent lights of different shapes and sizes were hung on wooden posts and scattered about the grounds. They lit up Edison's house and the staff accommodation, and lined the sides of the street.

Stories spread of the mysterious lights at Menlo Park and visitors came to see the spectacle.

On New Year's Eve, 1879, Edison held an official exhibition for hundreds of people, including reporters and celebrities.

"Soon we'll light up New York City," he proudly declared, "and then the world."

Everyone was amazed. It seemed as if each light bulb held a tiny glowing fire inside.

The London *Times* reported that the light was "bright, clear, mellow, regular, free from flickering or pulsations . . . better than gas, more regular, and emitting so small heat no danger exists from fire."

The press and public were enchanted with Edison's light project and money poured in from investors to support his work.

Publicity
Edison knew that support from the press and the public was important for the success of his electric lighting system.

Lighting up the world

1880 Edison hired more laboratory assistants to help him improve his basic light system. He continued searching for a stronger, longer-lasting filament than the carbonised thread. At last, carbonised bamboo proved successful. Edison sent an assistant to Japan to organise a shipment of the bamboo, and in October 1880, he set up a factory to manufacture incandescent lamps.

Incandescent lamp factory
By 1892, Edison's factory produced four million light bulbs per year. By 1903, 45 million light bulbs per year were being produced. This picture shows some of the factory workers in 1910.

During these experiments, Edison noticed carbon deposits on the insides of the glass bulbs. He proved that these deposits were made by electrical charges inside the bulb. This was called the "Edison effect", and later became the basis of electronic machines.

But Edison remained focused on his electric light system.

"We'll need to distribute electricity from the power plant to homes and other buildings," he thought. "But the electricity supply must stay constant no matter how near or far the buildings are from the power station."

With the help of a model grid dug into the grounds at Menlo Park, he devised a network of underground cables and wires that was not only efficient but also saved money.

Now, Edison was ready to light up New York.

Edison effect
Edison did not see a practical use for an electric current given off by the filament inside a light bulb. However, in 1904, John Fleming invented the vacuum tube (shown above) – a device that controls the flow of electric charges (electrons) – based on this Edison effect. This marked the beginning of electronics.

Downtown New York
The area marked out for Edison's light system was part of the Wall Street financial district. This included the New York Stock Exchange where Edison had his first inventing success.

Workforce
Many of the people who helped build Edison's electric light system came to America from other countries. More than 5.2 million immigrants entered the United States between 1880 and 1890.

1881 Soon, Edison received permission to install his electric light system in a square mile of downtown New York City. He moved back to the city temporarily to oversee the work. He chose a large abandoned building on Pearl Street for the site of the central power station.

Workers dug trenches in the roads for the cables. They installed wires, sockets and fittings for every light in every building to be lit up.

Sketch from a magazine showing cables being laid

They also installed meters so that once the system was running, the Edison Electric Illuminating Company could measure the amount of electricity used at each building and charge a fee for it.

Headquarters Edison moved his offices to this mansion in New York City. This was a far cry from his arrival ten years earlier as a penniless inventor.

People were excited about Edison's new light system, but also nervous. Was there some sort of magic in the cables beneath their feet? Was it dangerous?

Meanwhile, Edison staged an exhibit at the International Electrical Exhibition in Paris. Orders began coming

in from Europe, and Edison opened the world's first commercial power station for incandescent lighting in London in April 1882.

Power station
Inside Edison's Pearl Street power station were four huge boilers, six steam engines and three enormous generators called "jumbos", named after a circus elephant.

Hydroelectricity
Edison was also a pioneer in hydroelectricity – the use of water power to generate electricity. Today, water power is harnessed by dams.

1882 In July, Edison finally tested the electric light system in New York City.

A witness at the power station observed, "It was a terrifying experience . . . The engines and dynamos made a horrible racket and the place seemed to be filled with sparks and flames of all colours."

To fix this problem, Edison synchronised the engines to run at the same speed. On September 4, he was ready to try again. He was unsure of the outcome, so he only invited a few reporters. At three o'clock that afternoon, he flicked the switch and the lights went on.

That evening, as the lights became more visible against the darkening sky, the press and public noticed the difference. The *New York Times* reported that taking notes beneath the lights "seemed almost like writing by daylight."

Gradually, towns across the United States and Europe began installing Edison's electric light system. Edison staged publicity stunts to increase enthusiasm. Sadly, Edison's wife, Mary, died in 1884, just as his electric light system was becoming popular.

Publicity stunts
The stunts Edison planned included hiring 400 men to wear light bulbs on their heads and an entertainer to tap-dance on an electrified floor wearing a helmet that flashed in time to the dance. The stunts helped sales. By 1887, Edison had opened 121 power stations in the United States and Europe.

Sounds and pictures

1885 Edison began seeing Mina Miller, the daughter of another inventor, and a year later, he proposed to her using Morse code. They had three children, Madeleine, Charles and Theodore. Edison moved the family to a mansion in West Orange, New Jersey. Nearby, he built a large new laboratory with "facilities superior to any other for rapid and cheap development of an invention." There was also factory space for manufacturing his inventions.

By the time the new laboratory opened in 1887, Edison had turned his attention back to the phonograph. Over the past decade, other inventors, such as Alexander Graham Bell, had improved Edison's phonograph. Now Edison set about making his own improvements.

Family photo
This picture shows Edison with Mina and their children. Mina tried to turn Edison into a refined, well dressed public figure.

Glenmont
When Edison bought this mansion in New Jersey, he said, "It's a great deal too nice for me, but it isn't half nice enough for my wife."

He added an electric motor and developed a new, reusable wax cylinder. He also invented a talking doll, with nursery rhymes playing on a tiny cylinder inside.

During the early 1890s, Edison recognised the potential of the phonograph for home entertainment. He began producing prerecorded cylinders of music to play on home phonographs. It was the beginning of the music recording industry.

Famous voices
Edison asked famous people of the day to record messages on the phonograph. Some of these recordings can still be heard, including the voices of Queen Victoria and Edison himself.

Record discs
In 1887, Emile Berliner invented a flat disc to be played on a phonograph. The disc could be played for longer than the cylinder and the sound was clearer.

Edison launched a huge advertising campaign for his phonograph.

Zoopraxiscope
Muybridge's invention had a picture disc that rotated to show each picture in quick sequence.

Moving pictures
The brain briefly continues to see an image after it disappears. When two pictures appear in quick succession, as in a flip book, the images overlap in the brain, making the pictures appear to move.

1888 Edison was fascinated when he watched a display of inventor Eadweard Muybridge's zoopraxiscope, which projected a series of photographs onto a screen. The horse in the photographs looked as if it was actually moving.

This was the first device to use photography to depict motion. It inspired Edison to create "an instrument that does for the eye what the phonograph does for the ear, which is the recording and reproduction of things in motion . . ."

Edison and engineer William Dickson experimented with a series of photographs on a rotating cylinder.

Part of the series of photographs of a horse running used by Muybridge for his zoopraxiscope

In 1889, French photographer Etienne Marey showed Edison how he used a reel of film in his camera to take many photographs in quick succession. Edison and Dickson made a film reel using a flexible film called celluloid that had recently been invented by George Eastman. They made holes in the sides of the film reel and tiny toothed wheels to move the film along – both ideas taken from Edison's earlier inventions. Motion pictures were now a reality.

Photographic plates
Until Eastman invented celluloid film, most still cameras recorded each image onto a rigid plate.

Silent movies
Edison and Dickson tried but failed to synchronise moving pictures with sound so they focused on silent films.

Peephole

Kinetoscope
At kinetoscope parlours, rows of wooden cabinets had kinetoscopes like this one inside.

The Big Sneeze
William Dickson produced many of the peep shows made at Edison's studio. One of the most famous peep shows featured mechanic Fred Ott sneezing.

1892 Edison and Dickson invented two motion-picture devices. The kinetograph was the first film camera. The kinetoscope was a viewer with a peephole used to watch motion pictures.

Edison decided that instead of projecting motion pictures onto a screen, he could make more money by opening amusement arcades called kinetoscope parlours. He then charged a fee for every 90-second peep show viewed on one of the arcade's many kinetoscopes. In the next few years, kinetoscope parlours became a popular form of entertainment in the United States and Europe.

In order to film the peep shows, Edison built a small motion picture studio on the grounds of his West Orange laboratory in 1893.

The building was called the Black Maria. It rotated on a track so it could

always capture the sunlight through a removable section of the roof.

Soon, musicians, actors, dancers, circus performers and other entertainers began coming to West Orange to be in short motion pictures filmed by Dickson. The film business had been born.

First film studio
Hundreds of short films were made at the Black Maria studio during the ten years it was open.

Kinetophone
In 1895, Edison introduced the kinetophone, which linked a kinetoscope with a phonograph inside the cabinet. The moving pictures and sound were still not synchronised.

Edison's endless ideas

Iron ore
Iron ore is used to make steel, machinery and many household items. Edison set up this large iron-ore mine at Ogdensberg, New Jersey.

X-rays
Edison's medical X-ray machine was first used on a patient with a bullet wound in his hand. Modern X-rays are vital for diagnosing many medical conditions.

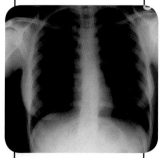

Although Edison had great success with the phonograph and kinetoscope, his real interest at the time was in processing iron ore. He spent more than ten years and several million dollars developing a process using magnets to separate valuable iron ore from ordinary rock. However, when vast supplies of iron ore were discovered in 1898, his business failed.

Discouraged but not defeated, Edison had many more ideas to pursue. A few years later, he recycled some of the iron-ore machinery for use in a cement-processing business.

In 1896, Edison experimented with X-rays, a form of electromagnetic energy which had recently been discovered. He put this technology to practical use by creating the first medical X-rays.

Henry Ford, the car manufacturer, became one of Edison's closest friends. Edison experimented with a storage battery to power electric cars. Although petrol became the standard power for cars instead of electricity, Edison's storage battery had many other uses and was the forerunner of today's alkaline battery. It was the most successful product of his later life.

Storage battery
In a storage battery, a chemical reaction produces an electric current. Putting electricity from another source into the battery reverses the reaction and recharges the battery for later use.

Edison in the back seat of a Model T driven by Henry Ford

Goldenrod
Edison used a variety of goldenrod that grew to 3.6 metres (12 feet) high. He extracted the rubber latex and made four Firestone tyres for a Ford car.

Camping trips
During his 60s and 70s, Edison enjoyed several camping trips with Ford, Firestone and other friends and celebrities of the time.

1914 Over the years, Edison formed many companies to manufacture his inventions. During World War I (1914-1918), he advised the United States Navy on military technology.

In 1927, Henry Ford and tyre manufacturer Harvey Firestone asked Edison to explore alternative sources of rubber for car tyres. Even at 80 years old, Edison enjoyed experimenting. After testing 17,000 plants, he found that rubber latex could be extracted from the goldenrod plant.

In 1929, the world celebrated the fiftieth anniversary of Edison's incandescent light bulb. Cities around the world put on special light displays to honour Edison and his invention.

Ford organised the Golden Jubilee of Light celebration at his new museum complex in Michigan, where he had rebuilt Edison's Menlo Park laboratory.

Edison re-enacted his breakthrough moment with the filament of carbonised thread.

"Let there be light!" he proclaimed, as the filament glowed inside the light bulb once again.

Though his legendary energy was fading, Edison was determined and persistent to the end. In 1931, he was still refining the processing of goldenrod rubber when he died, at the age of 84.

Menlo Park replica
To make the replica of the Menlo Park laboratory authentic, Ford even transported the soil from the old New Jersey site. When Edison saw the restored lab, he remarked, "We never kept it as clean as this!"

Edison's research into the recording of sound paved the way for modern CD players.

Research today
Companies now invest huge amounts into research and development. Teams of people work together to create things that we will use, just like Edison and his staff did in his labs.

Inventing the future

At the 1929 celebration for the Golden Jubilee of Light, Edison said, "In honouring me, you are also honouring that vast army of thinkers and workers of the past without whom my work would have gone for nothing."

Every invention is based at least in part on the research and experiments of a previous inventor. Certainly, without Edison's 1,093 inventions, we wouldn't have many of the things now often considered necessities – most significantly, an electric power supply at the flip of a switch.

One of Edison's key contributions was the research and development laboratory, where he and his staff turned ideas into practical products.

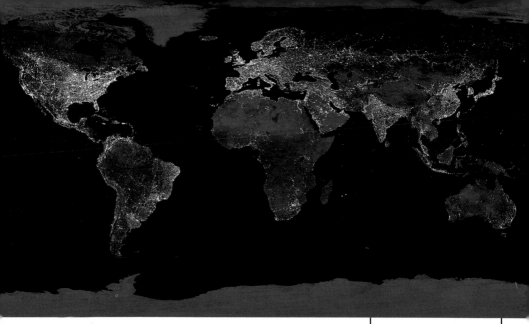

Photograph of Earth at night taken from space

In the same way, modern companies rely heavily on industrial research facilities to create new products to sell to the public.

Edison's impact on the world can be seen in the photograph above, which shows the concentration of electric lights on Earth. There are few places in the world that are not brightly lit.

Without a doubt, Edison's vision of a world transformed by his inventions certainly came true.

An electric world
In 1999, Thomas Edison topped the list of people who "made the millennium" in a survey by *Life* magazine. The magazine wrote, "Because of him, the millennium will end in a wash of brilliant light rather than in torchlit darkness as it began."

Glossary

Carbon
A non-metallic chemical element that has many different forms, such as charcoal, lampblack, diamond and graphite.

Cement
A substance containing lime and clay used to bind together the other ingredients in mortar and concrete.

Conductor
A substance that allows heat, sound, or electrical energy to pass through it.

Electric current
A flow of electricity caused by electrically charged particles moving in a certain direction.

Electronics
A technology that uses devices which control a flow of electrons (negatively charged electric particles) through a gas, vacuum, or semiconductor.

Exhibition
A display of people's work opened for the public to come and see.

Filament
A single thread made from a conductor used inside an electric light bulb.

Generator
A machine that changes mechanical energy into electricity.

Incandescent lamp
A bulb with a filament heated by an electric current so that it gives off bright white light.

Invention
A new device or process made or thought up through studying and experimenting.

Iron ore
A rock or mineral containing iron, a silver-white metal.

Kinetograph
The first film camera invented by Thomas Edison and William Dickson in 1892. The device had an electric motor that moved a roll of celluloid film past the camera lens, while taking separate still photographic frames of moving images.

Laboratory
A place equipped for scientific research and experimentation.

Particle
The tiniest possible part of a substance.

Phonograph
A device for recording and playing back sounds, invented by Thomas Edison in 1877.

Power station
A building with generators inside where electricity is made.

Receiver
The part of a communication system, such as a telephone, radio, or telegraph, that receives a signal sent by radio waves or by wire.

Telegraph
A system of communication in which electric signals are sent by wire from a transmitter to a receiver.

Transmitter
The part of a communication system, such as a telephone, radio, or telegraph, that sends a signal by radio waves or by wire.

Vacuum
An empty, enclosed space from which air and other substances have been removed.

X-ray
An invisible electromagnetic ray that can pass through solid substances.